WHIMSICAL BIRDS

sing

soar

dance

race

enrich

balance

hang in

jump

stand tall

land

nurture

WHIMSICAL BIRDS
Sue Lewis

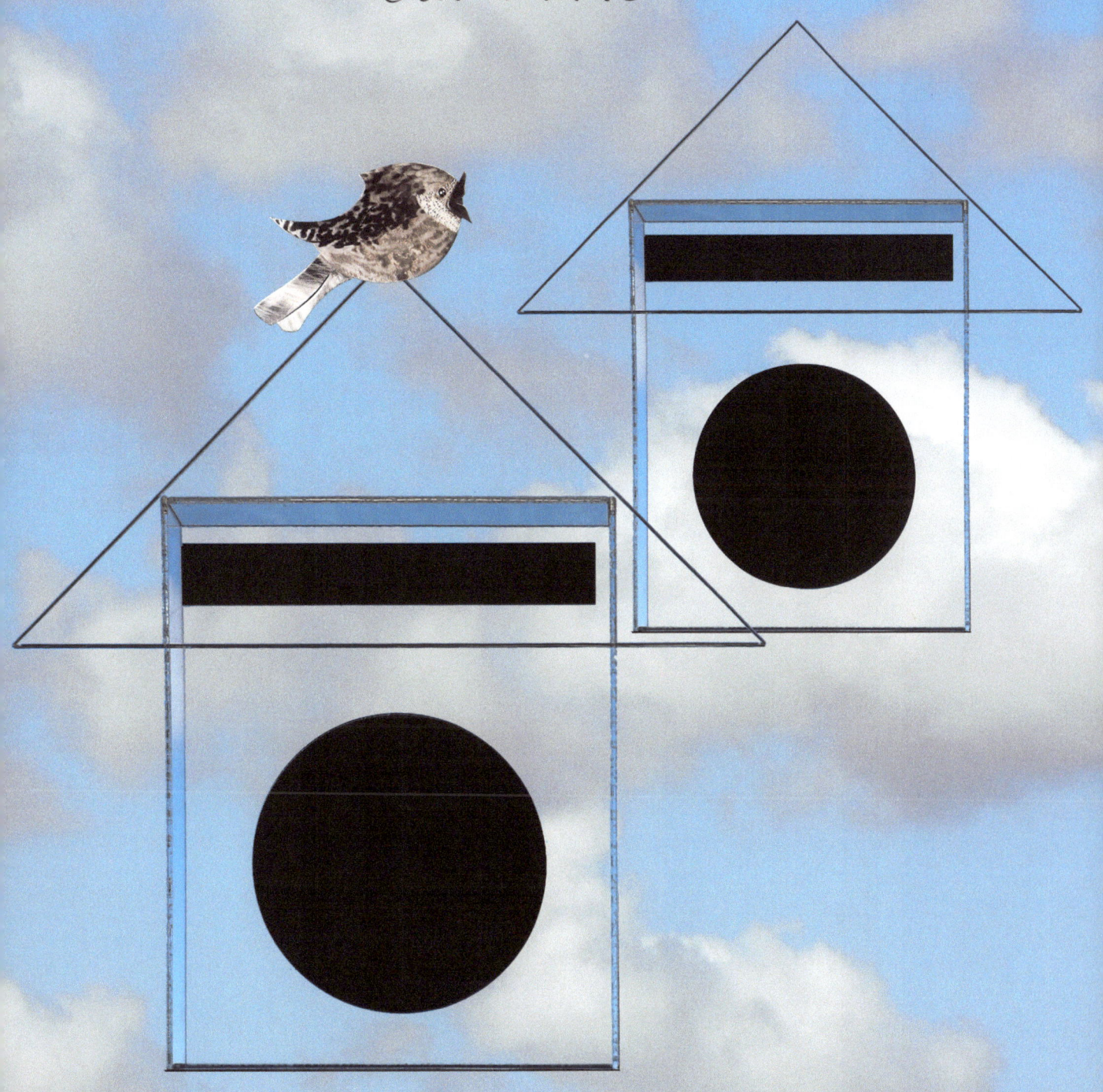

Whimsical Birds

Cover and technical design by Heinz Kagerer

Printed in the United States of America

Artist's Mission Statement

In a world surrounded by
Power struggles, poverty, and greed,
My art work aims not be a naive response
To this negative energy, but rather to carry
A contrasting positive gentle sensibility.

Acknowledging goodness over evil begins
For me in being with the stories in nature.
The dancing leaves,
Somersaulting clouds,
And singing cardinals become reminders
-- Along with the rapture and awe of children --
That we live where we are
Not only in geography but also in spirit.

My work aims to speak from this place
Of respect for nature and love for
The childlike wonder and whimsy.
One by one each piece has been
Thoughtfully conceived and tenderly created
As a peaceful pause with respect for
The sacred in the simple.

May you find joy
Through their unique visual voices.

About the Author

I am committed to truthful art. The voices of nature and our own stories are my funding forces. Technical skills become the carrier, not an end.

I consider myself an artistic problem solver creating poetic objects as my response to nature and the human condition. Balances reflected in the work include the whimsical with the spiritual, the technical with the metaphoric, and the personal with the universal. I am aware that the extraordinary is in the ordinary if we take time to be with it.

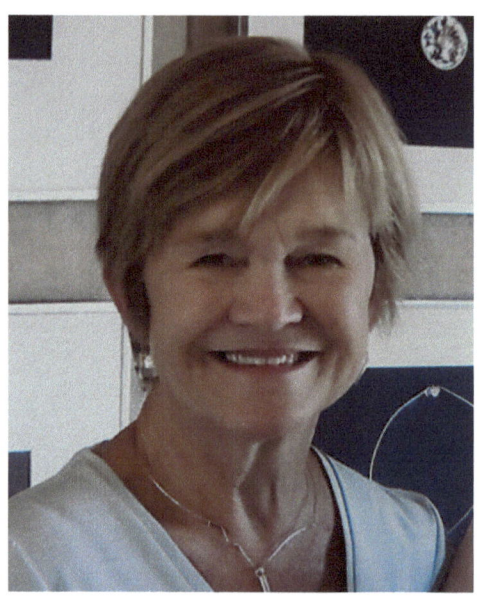

My education began in my mother's art studio where messing around was not only allowed but encouraged. My father's desire to see a more traditional direction led to an English lit focus with teaching certification, followed by art education certification and an M.A. in Designer Crafts and Painting—all from Iowa State University. Postgraduate work included course work in art therapy, counseling, and administrative endorsement plus numerous art and humanities workshops across the country. As a career art educator I taught for more than thirty years in public schools (primarily high school), Drake University as an adjunct art professor, teacher training workshops and at the Des Moines Art Center. I have had four solo shows in Iowa and have been carried by art galleries in Iowa, Colorado and Arizona. My artwork is an amalgamation of my life experiences. And as long as I am blessed with the ability to create, I will. I wish you joy in your own truth seeking. May this work prod a thought or two.

Sue Avery Lewis

Introduction

Are you lucky to be awakened by a chorus of birds? Have you listened carefully enough to discover the mindful messages each sings? Whether they whisper timidly or belt out the news confidently, the birds wish for you to enjoy the wisdom they share. All we need to do is listen -- very, very carefully. Here are a few tidbits I have observed:

Flying from branch to branch or saguaro to saguaro, the wren suggests, "Landing spots are a choice you make."
Observing a flock of birds shifting position in the formation, may invite us to ask, "What are the patterns that connect."
Or the grounded bird perched on the fence which appears to be wearing a backpack chirps, "It's tough to fly when you're overloaded."
And in this mode of thinking, his fine feather friend suggest as he sheds a feather or two, "Just let go" or "Keep it light," and takes off upward bound.
The wise old owl observes this interaction from his perch in the tree and thinks to himself, "Learning enriches the flight."
"Marching out from beneath a bush, the mommy quail leads the parade while twelve tiny babies scoot along single file with Daddy taking up the rear. It all demonstrates, "Survival seeks cooperation."
The roadrunner, luckily, sees the coyote lurking behind the brush. Using all of his physical resources he runs and flies out of reach just in time to report back, "Running away may be the only mode of survival."
In dialogue the turkey vulture, the hummingbird, and the flamingo share, "There is no one right answer."
Ah, the cardinal cheerfully reminds us, "Life is a series of short lived joys."

This body of artwork is based upon further noted messages. Enjoy these. And enjoy your own discoveries as you pay attention to the birds you encounter.

Each jewelry piece houses in a 14" x 14" x 1.25" acrylic home until brought out to be worn and to be enjoyed as a piece of wall art when not worn. The jewelry pieces range from 2" to 4" in width or height.

A collection of 16"x 20" watercolors mirror the thoughts and images of the silver series.

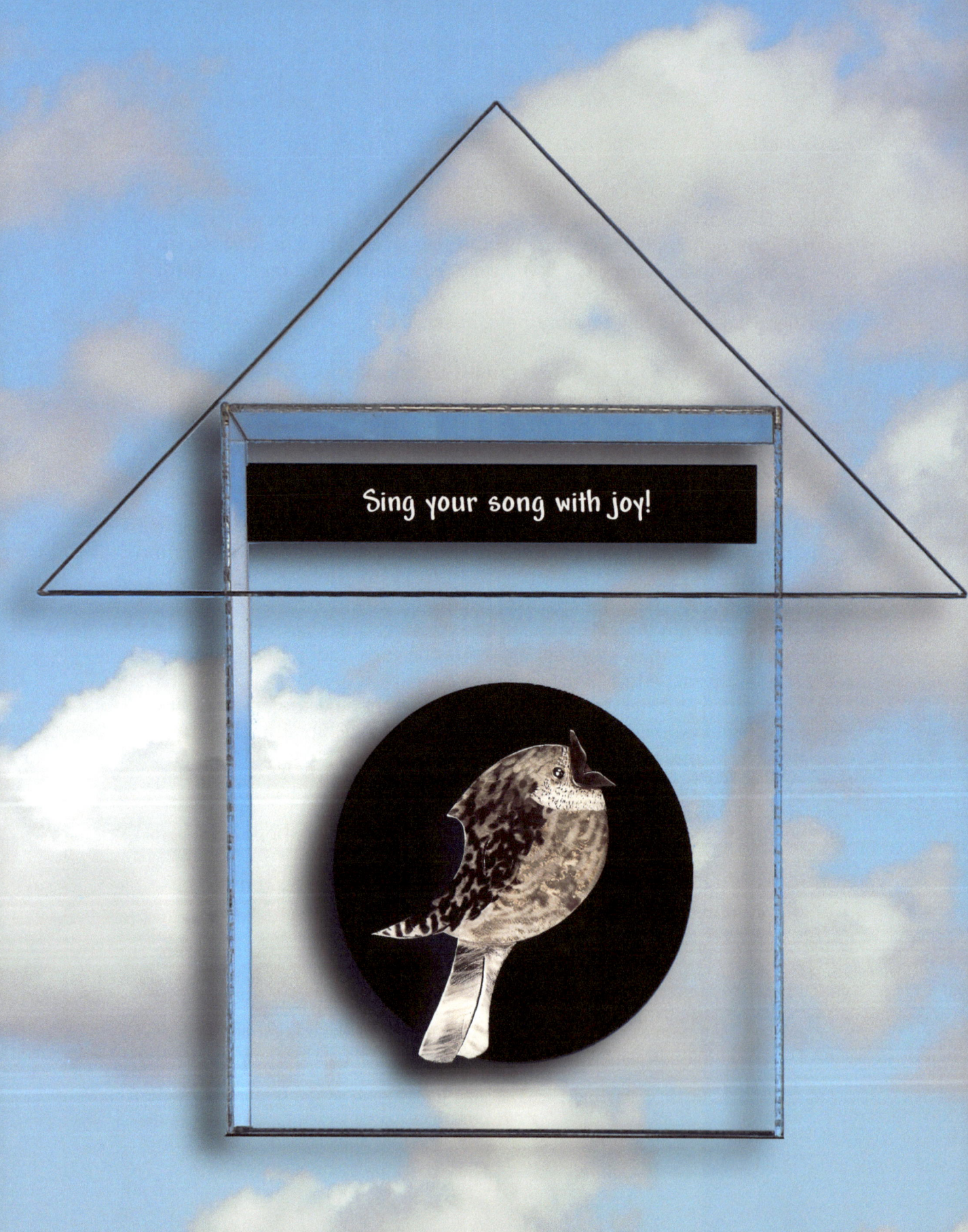

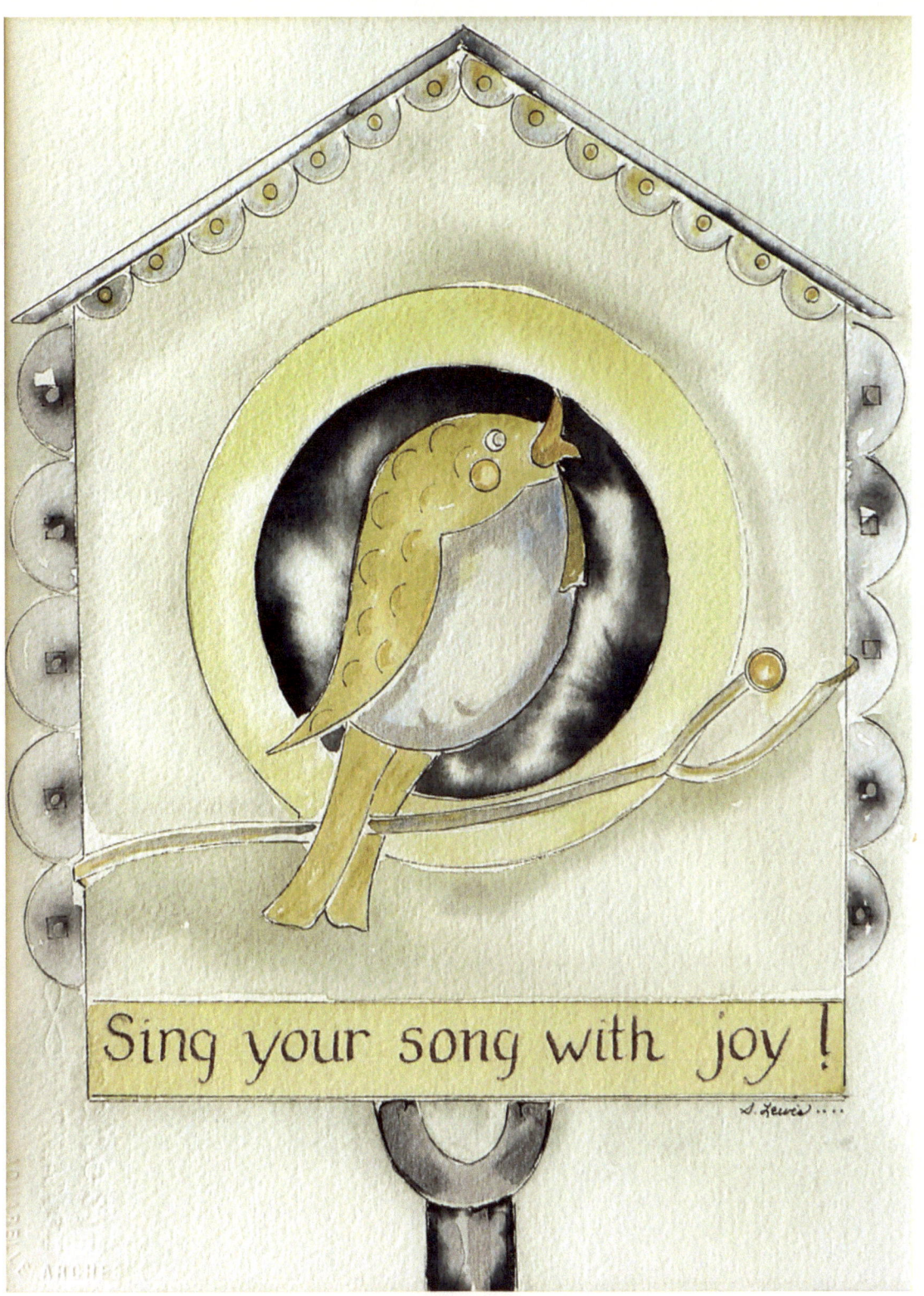

Sing your song with joy !

S. Lewis ....

Balance the flight!

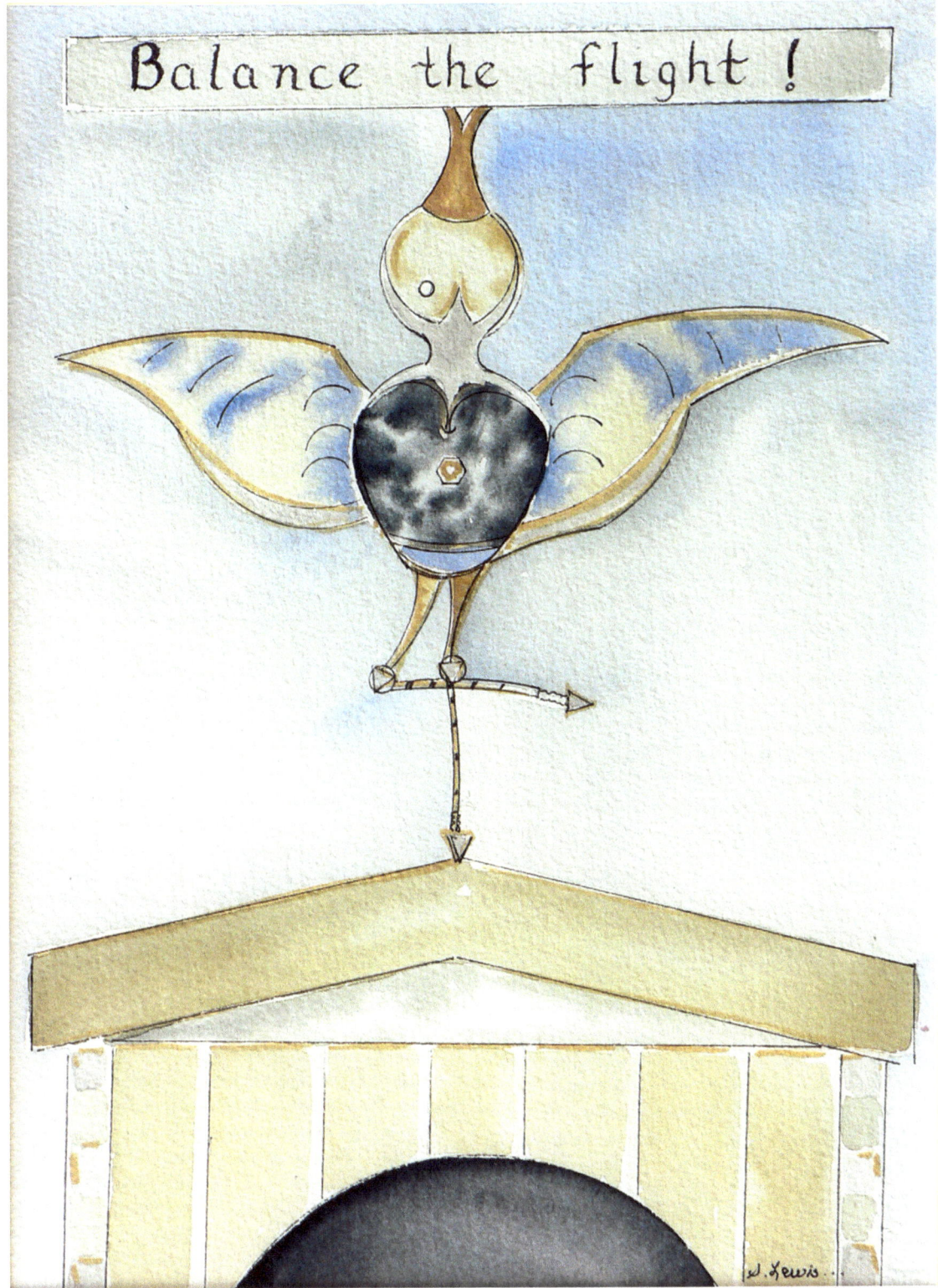

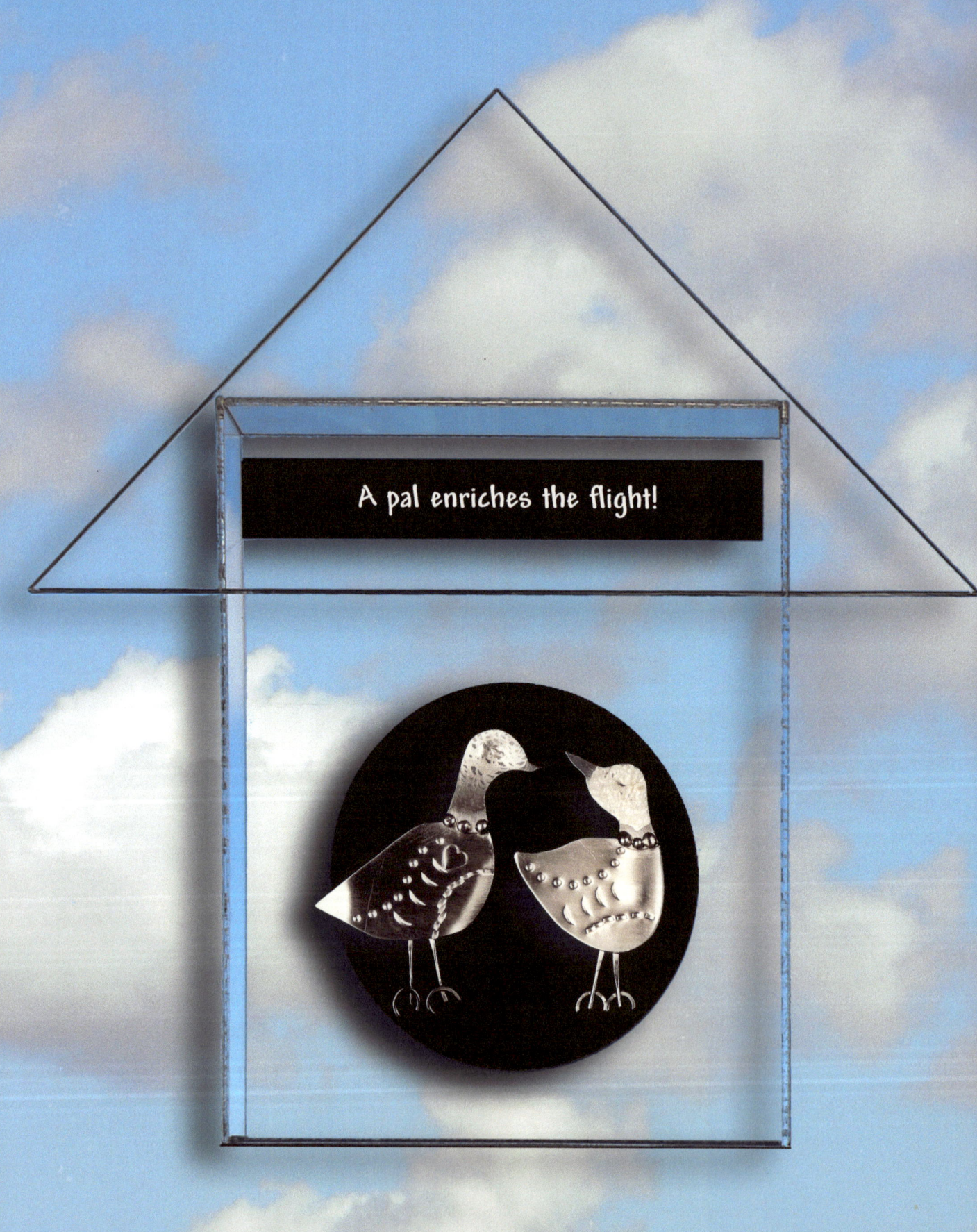

A pal enriches the flight!

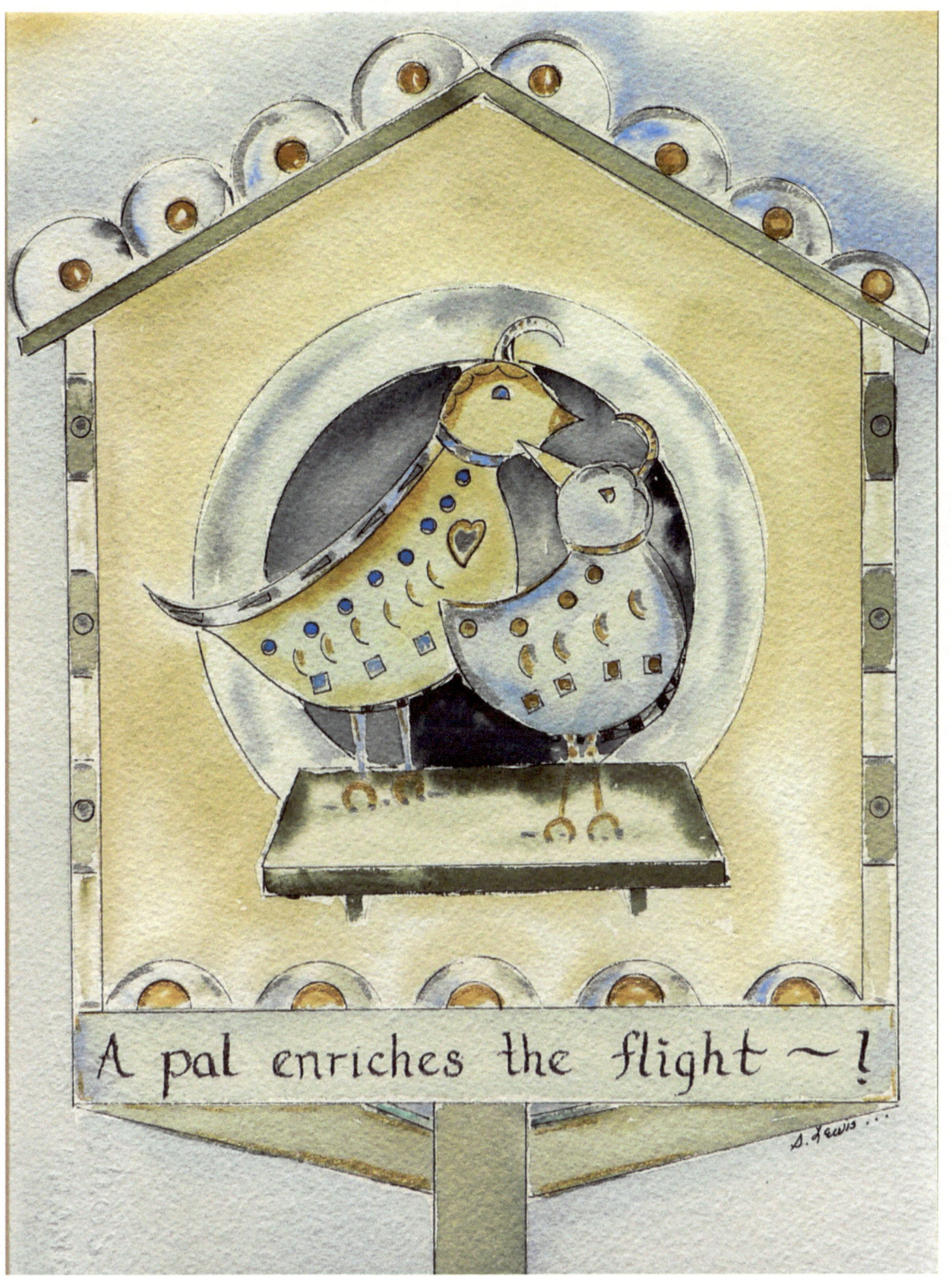

A pal enriches the flight ~ !

S. Lewis ...

Nurture your treasures!

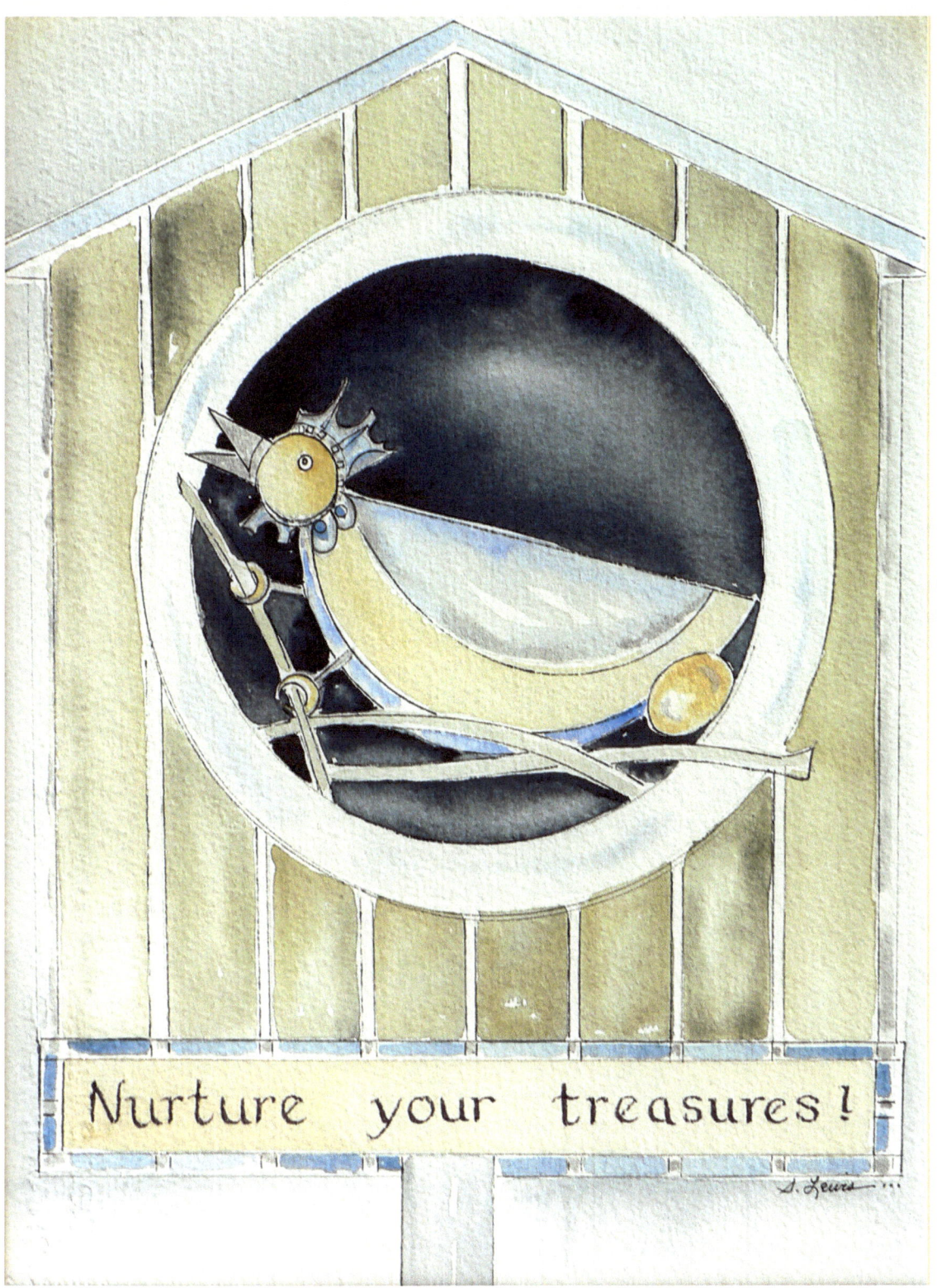

Nurture your treasures!

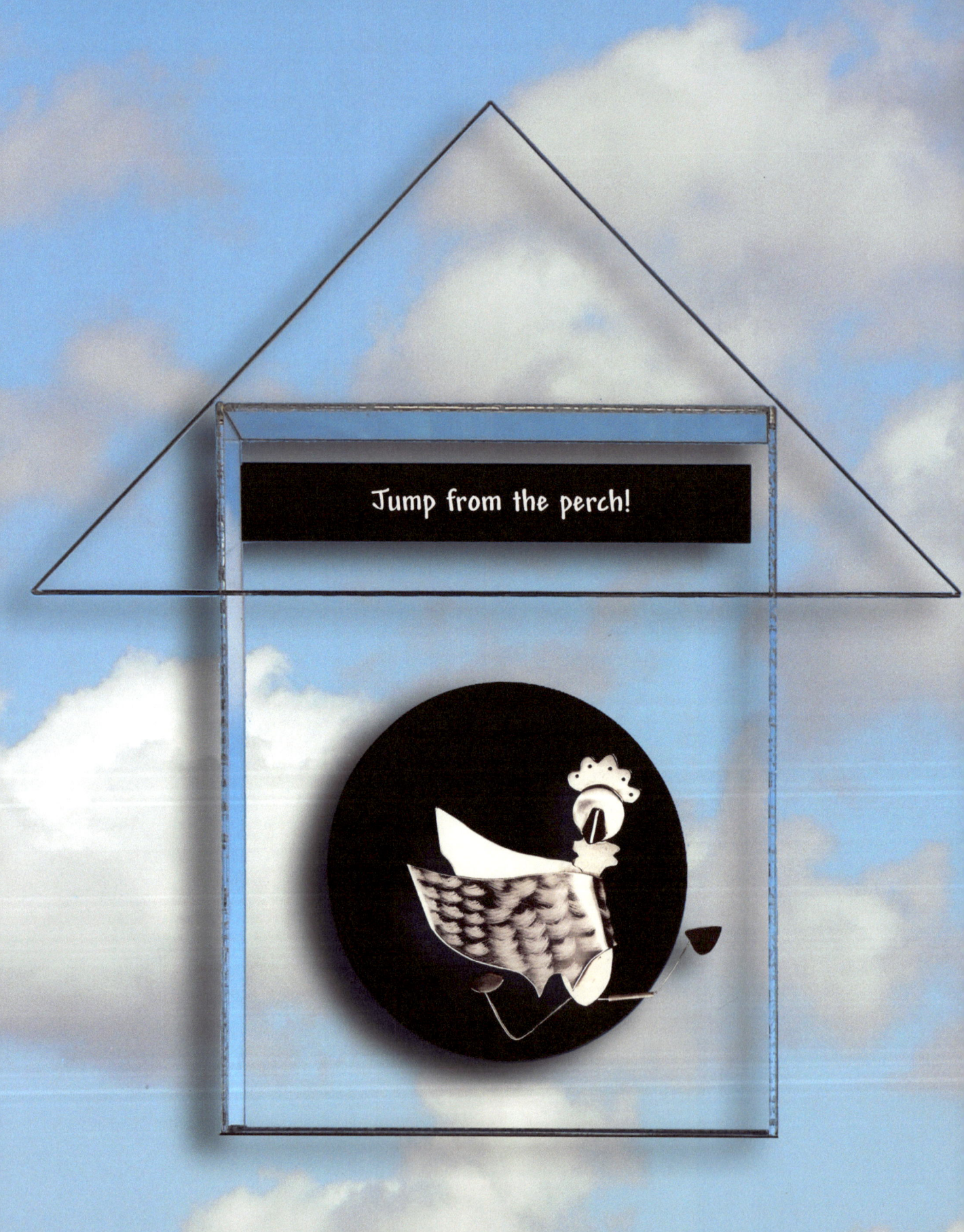

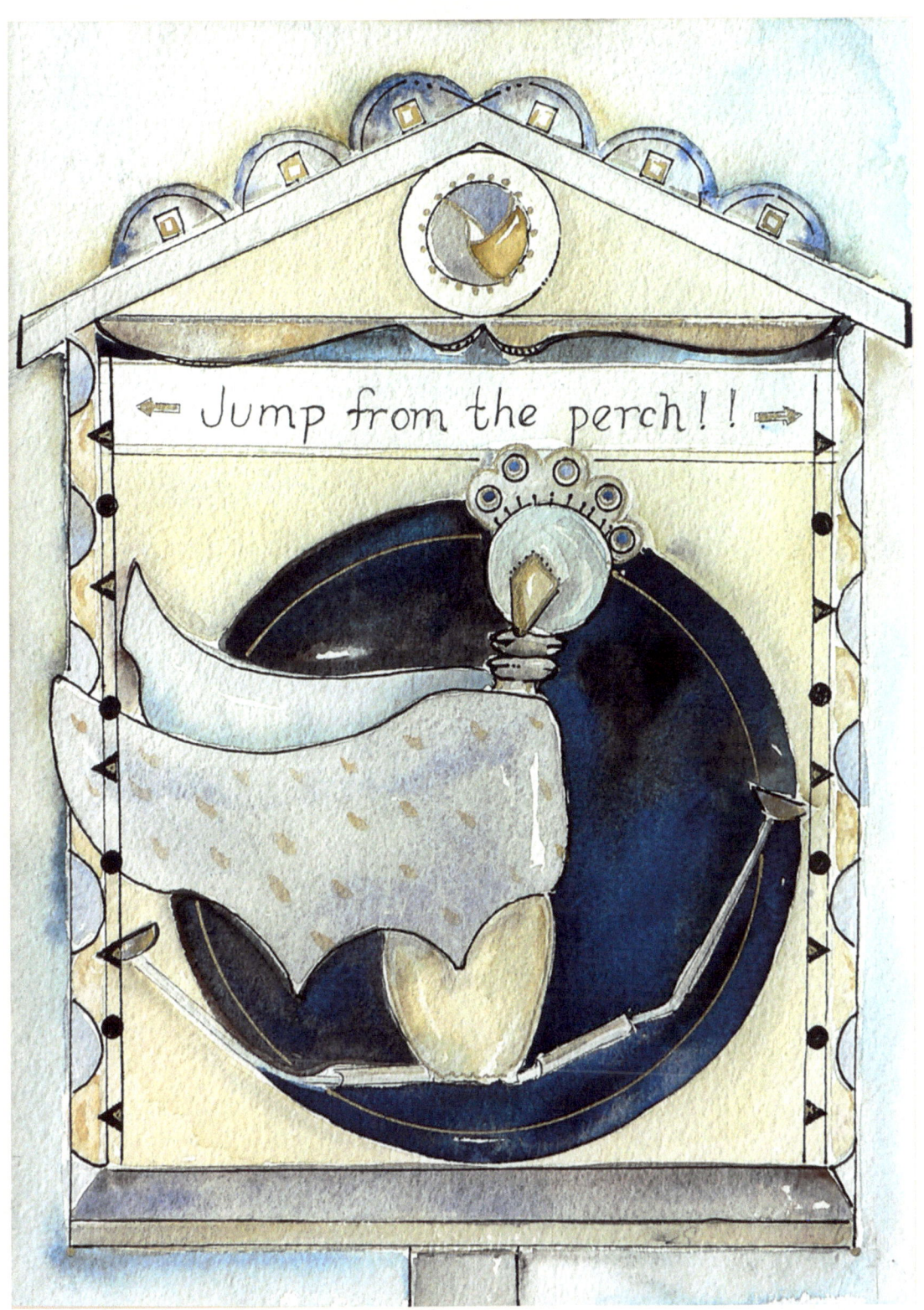

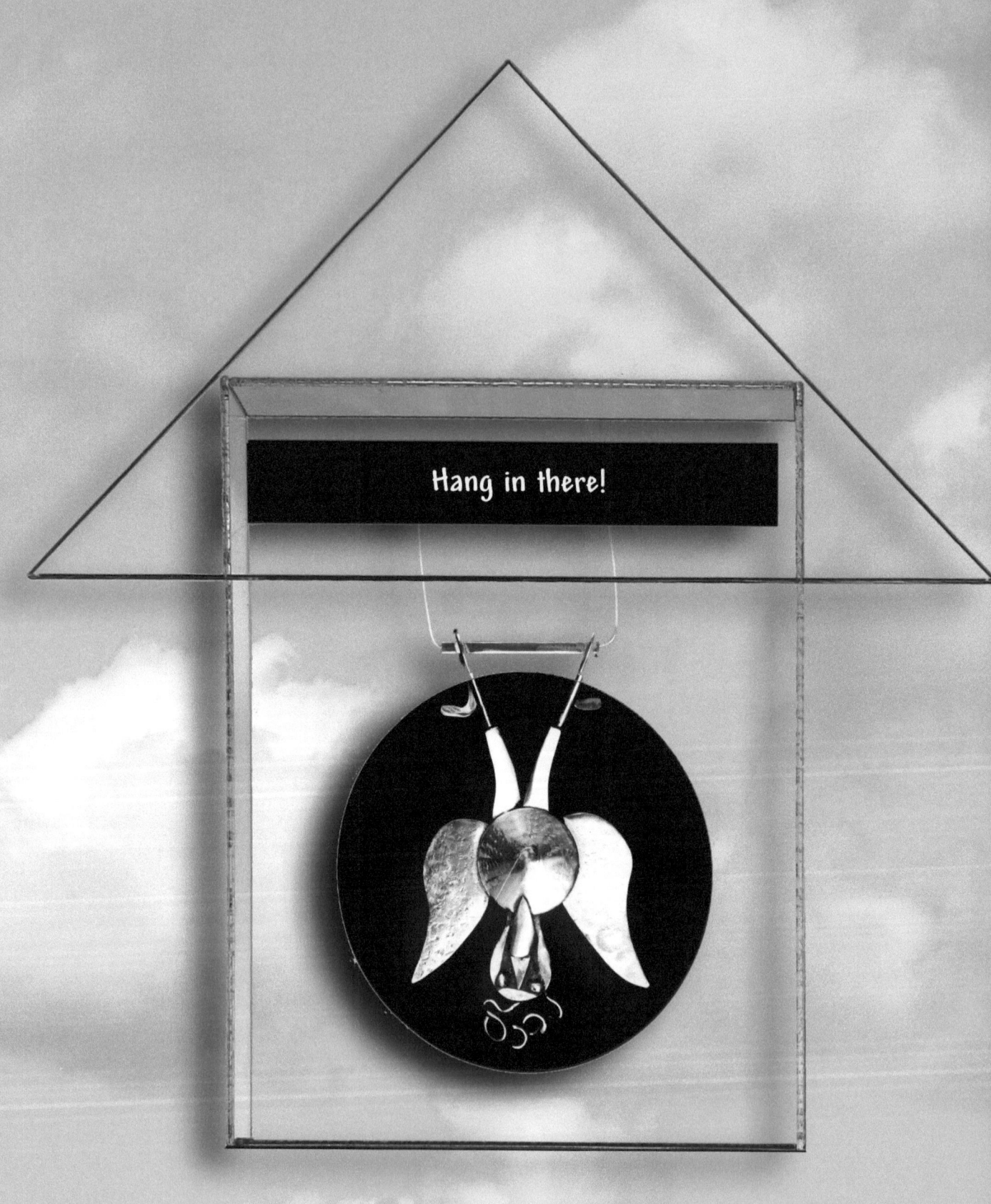

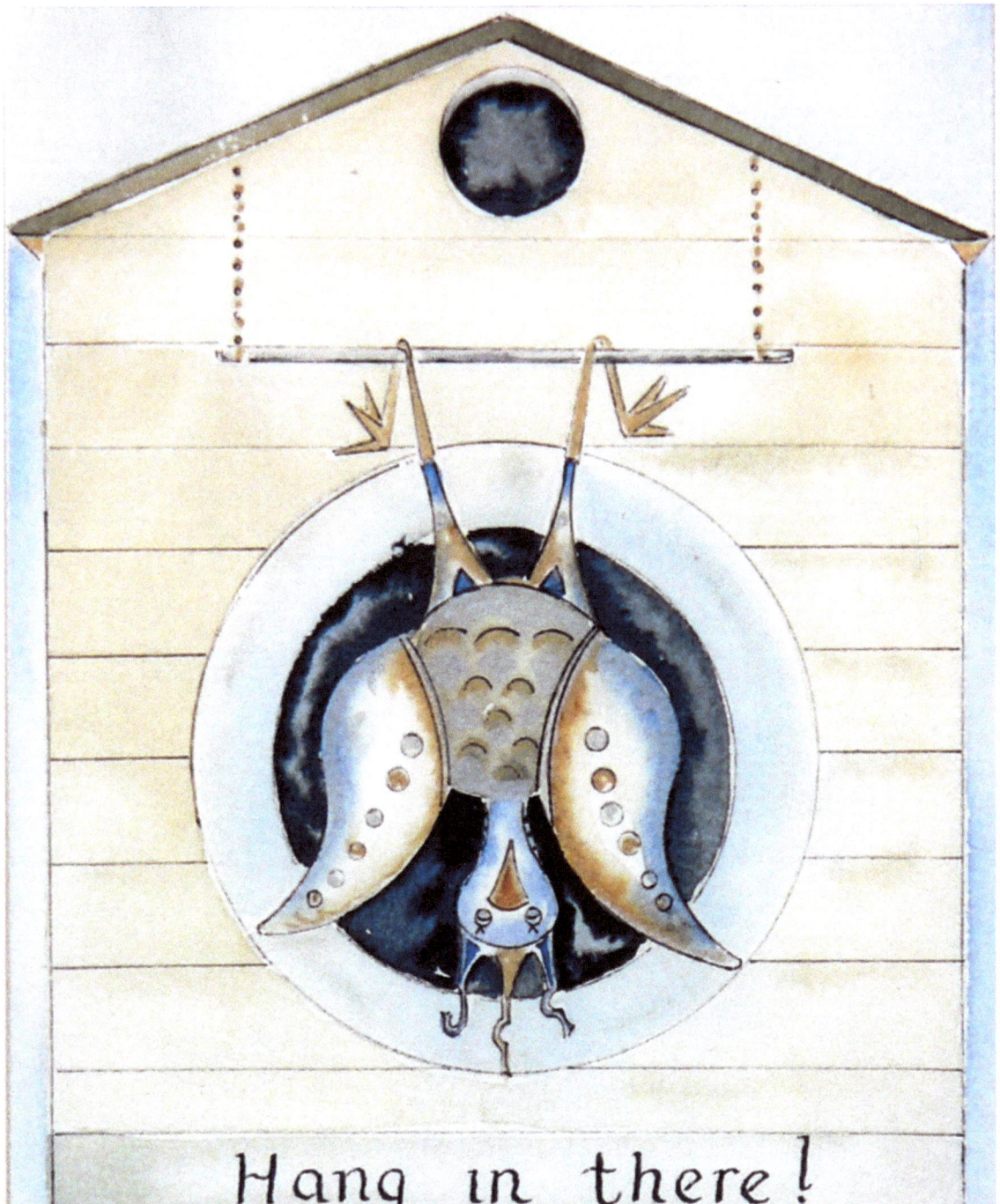

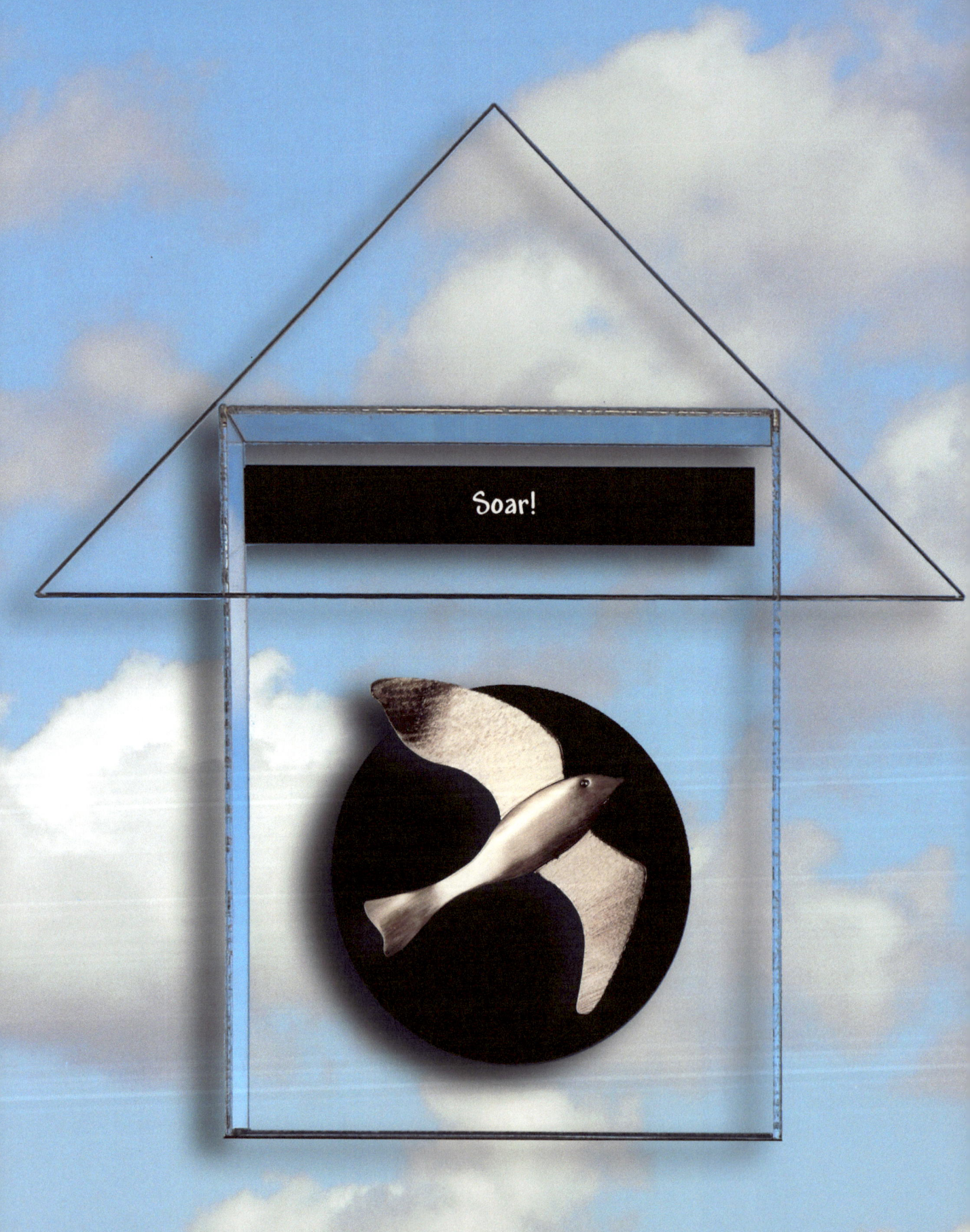

Soar!

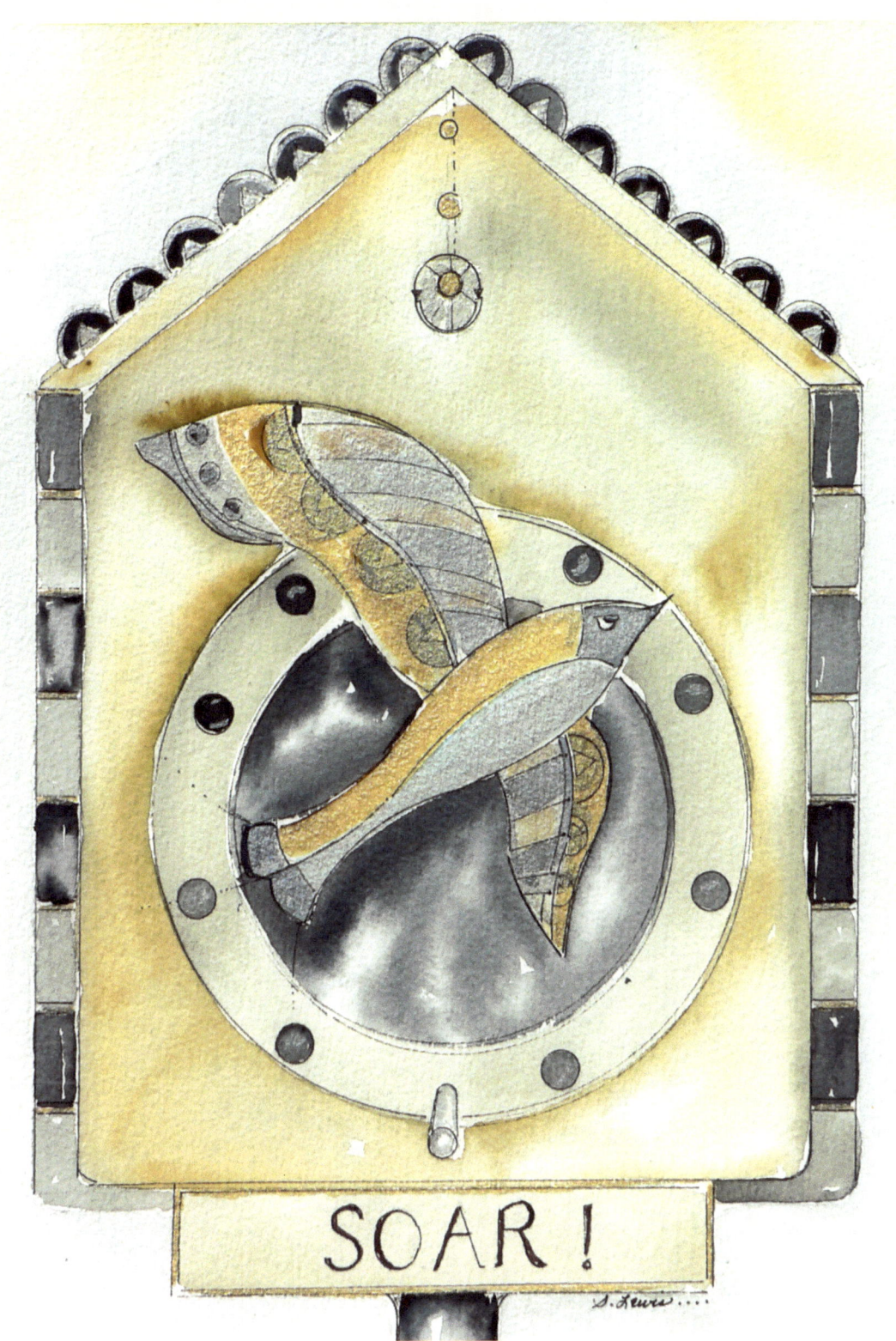

SOAR !

S. Lewis...

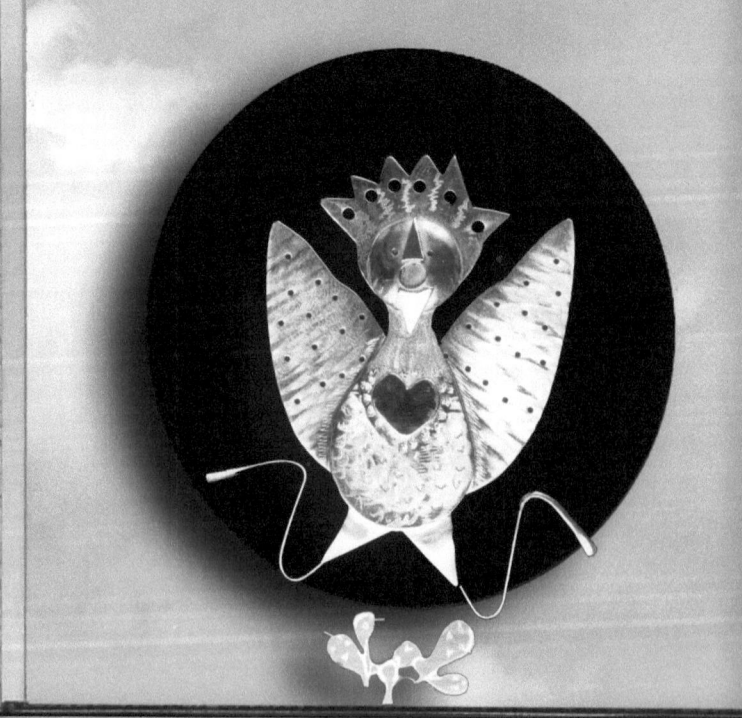

You don't always land where you plan!

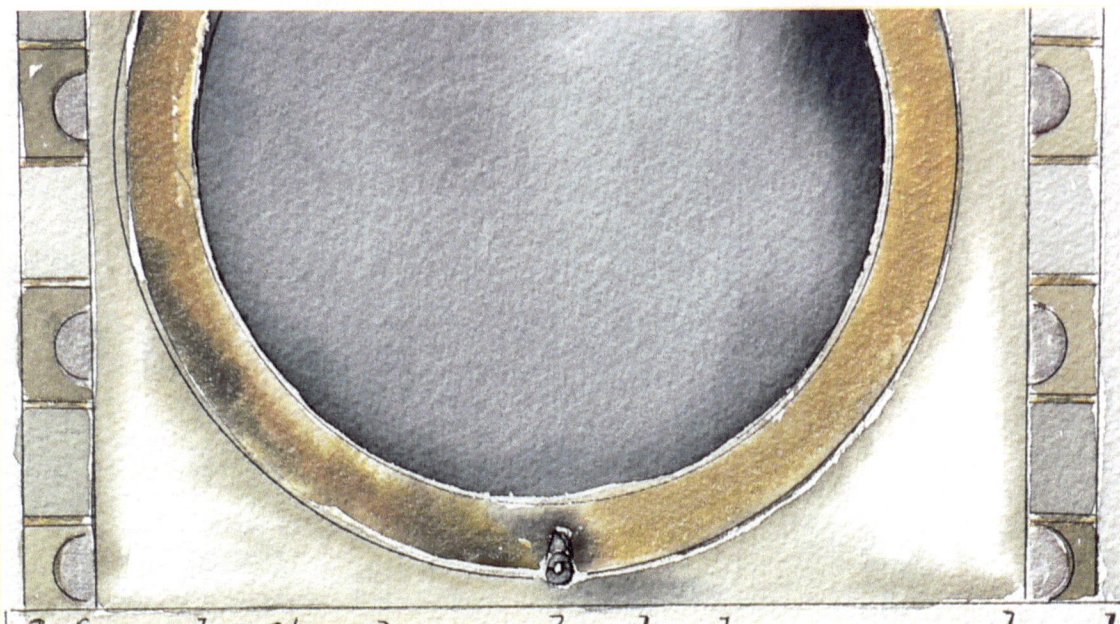

You don't always land where you plan!

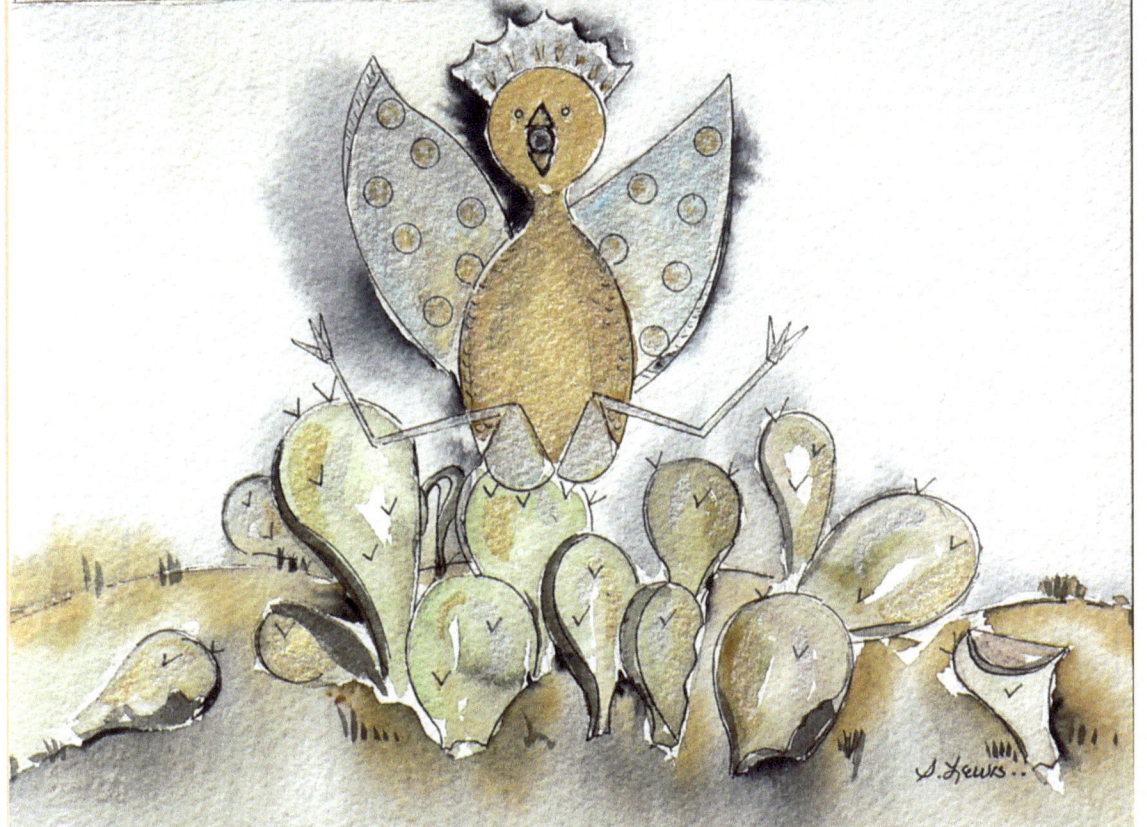

S. Lewis..

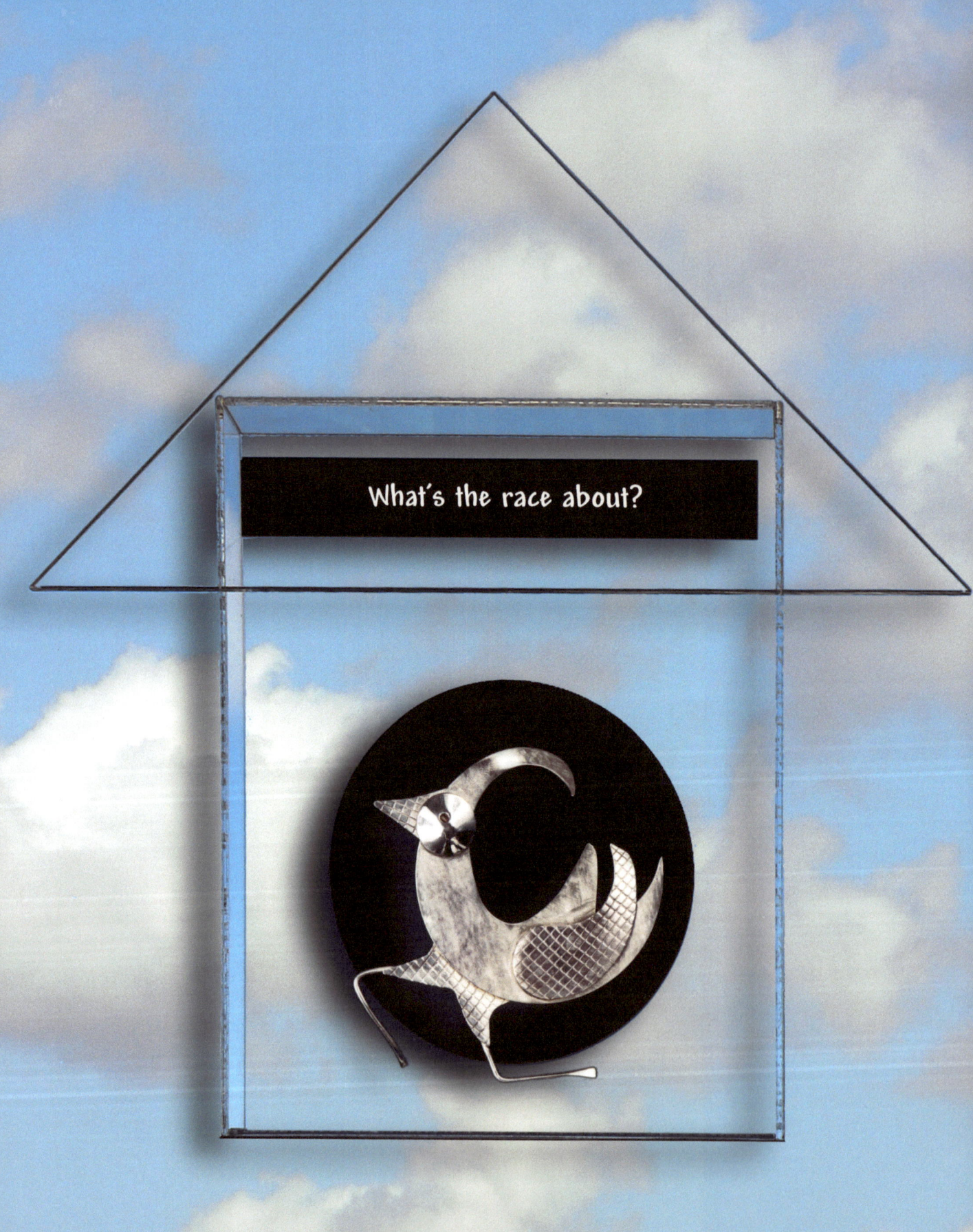

What's the race about?

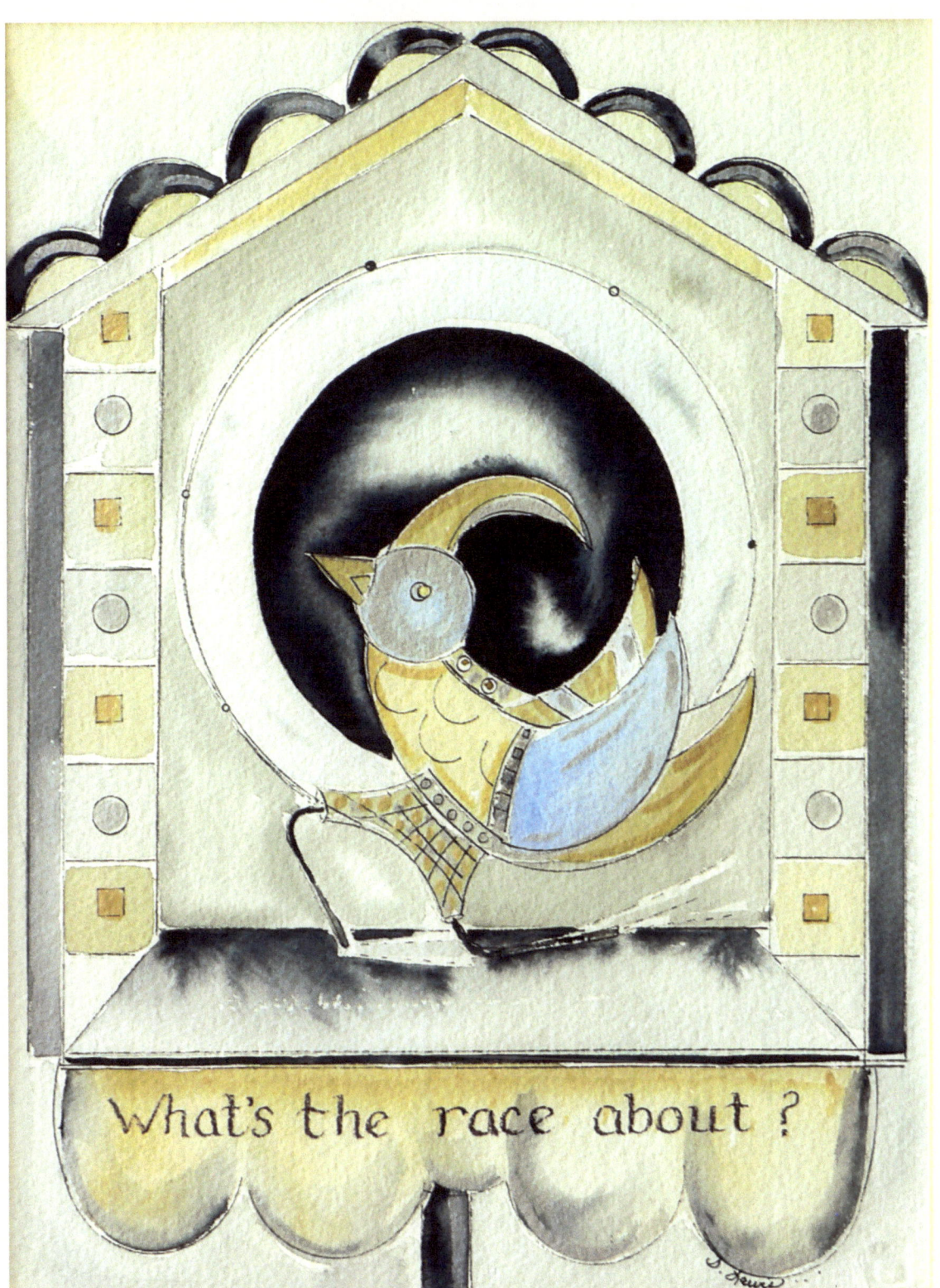

What's the race about ?

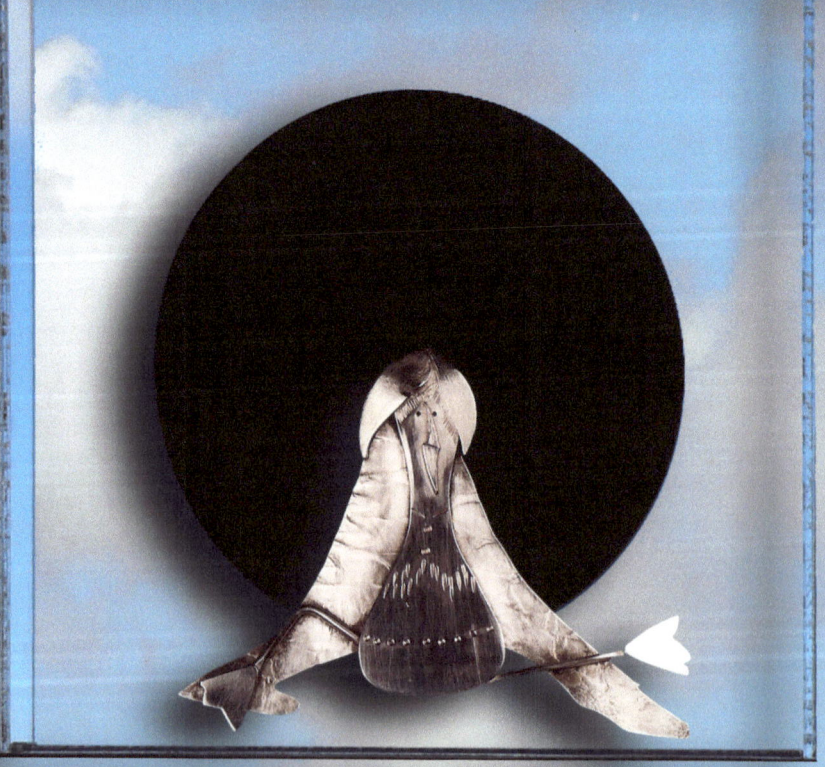

Sometimes you're just too tired for take off.

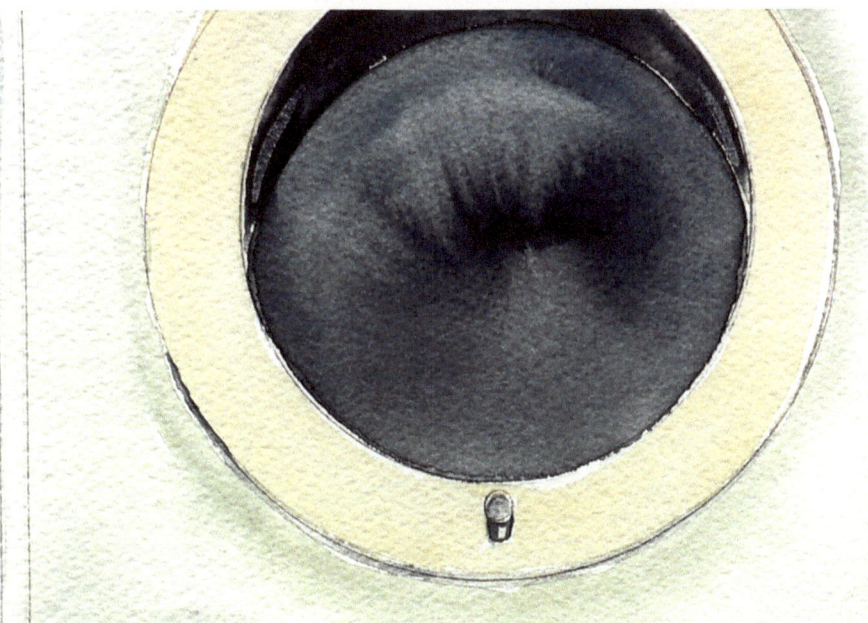

Sometimes you're just too tired for take off ...

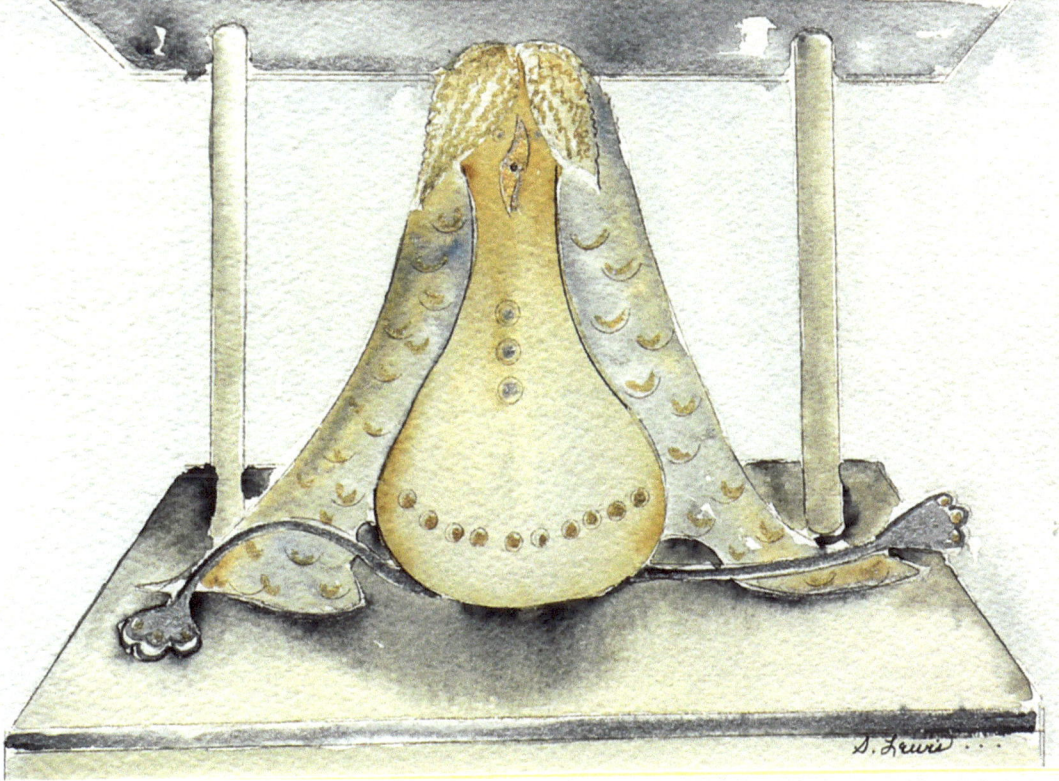

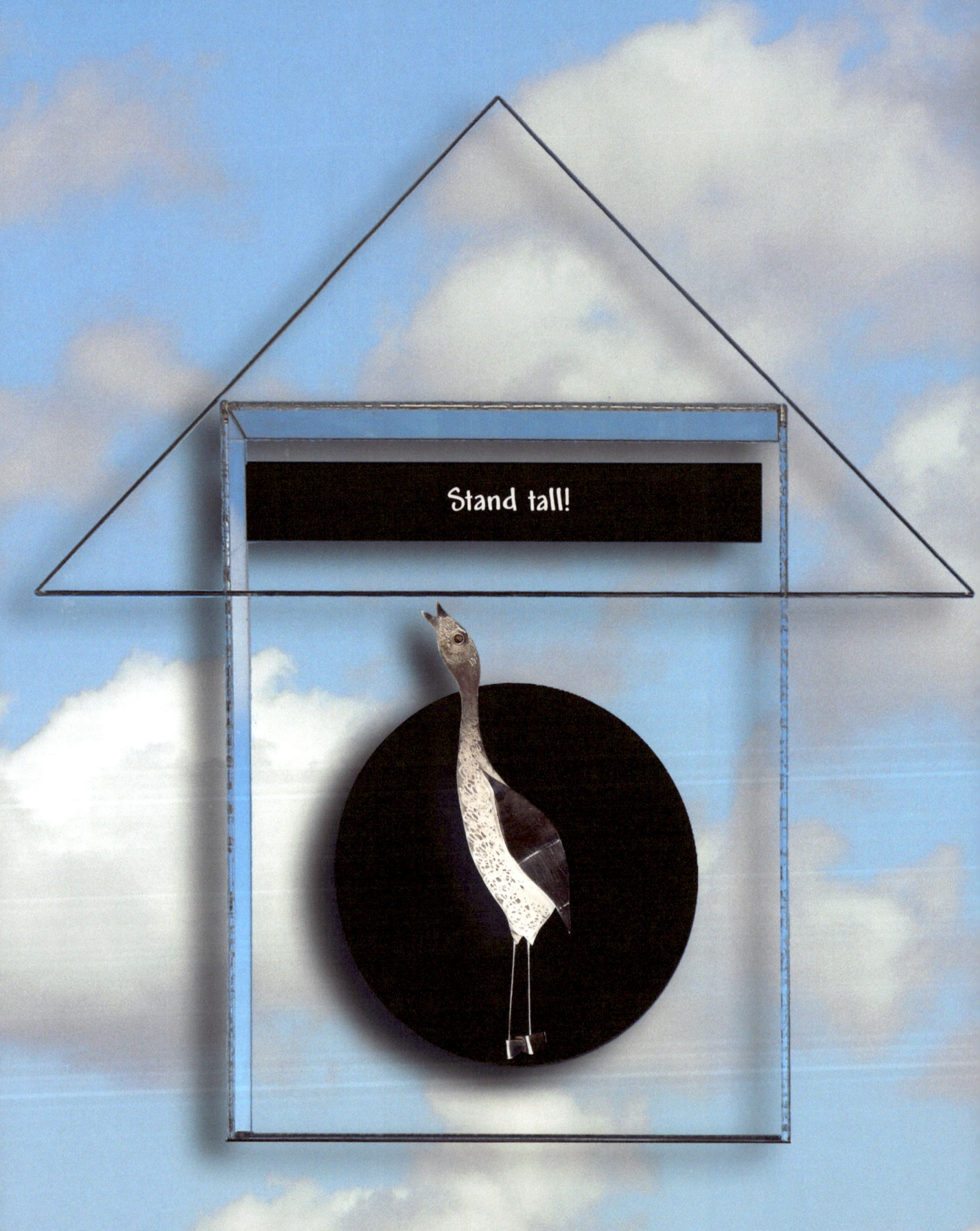

Stand tall!

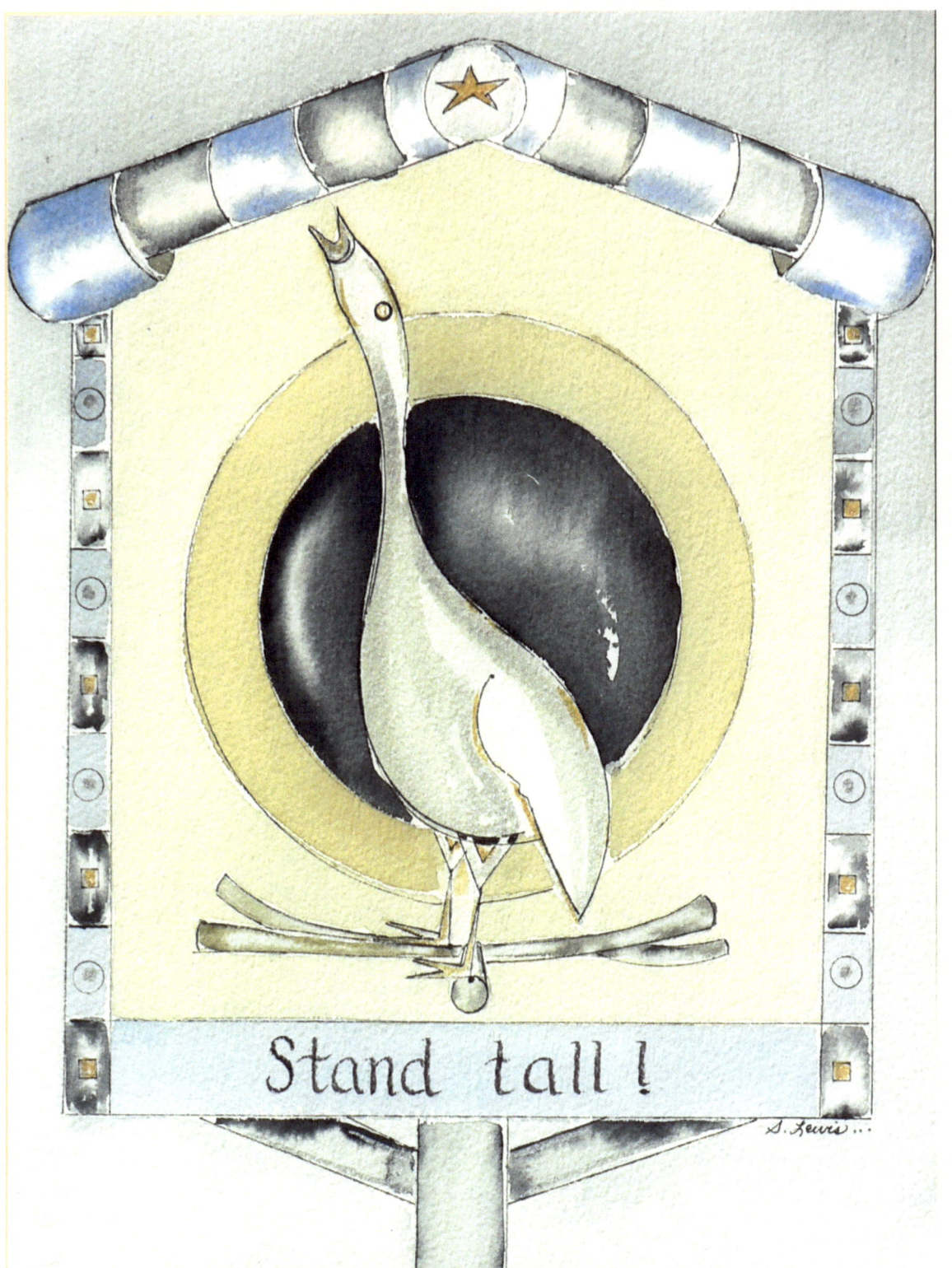

Stand tall !

S. Lewis...

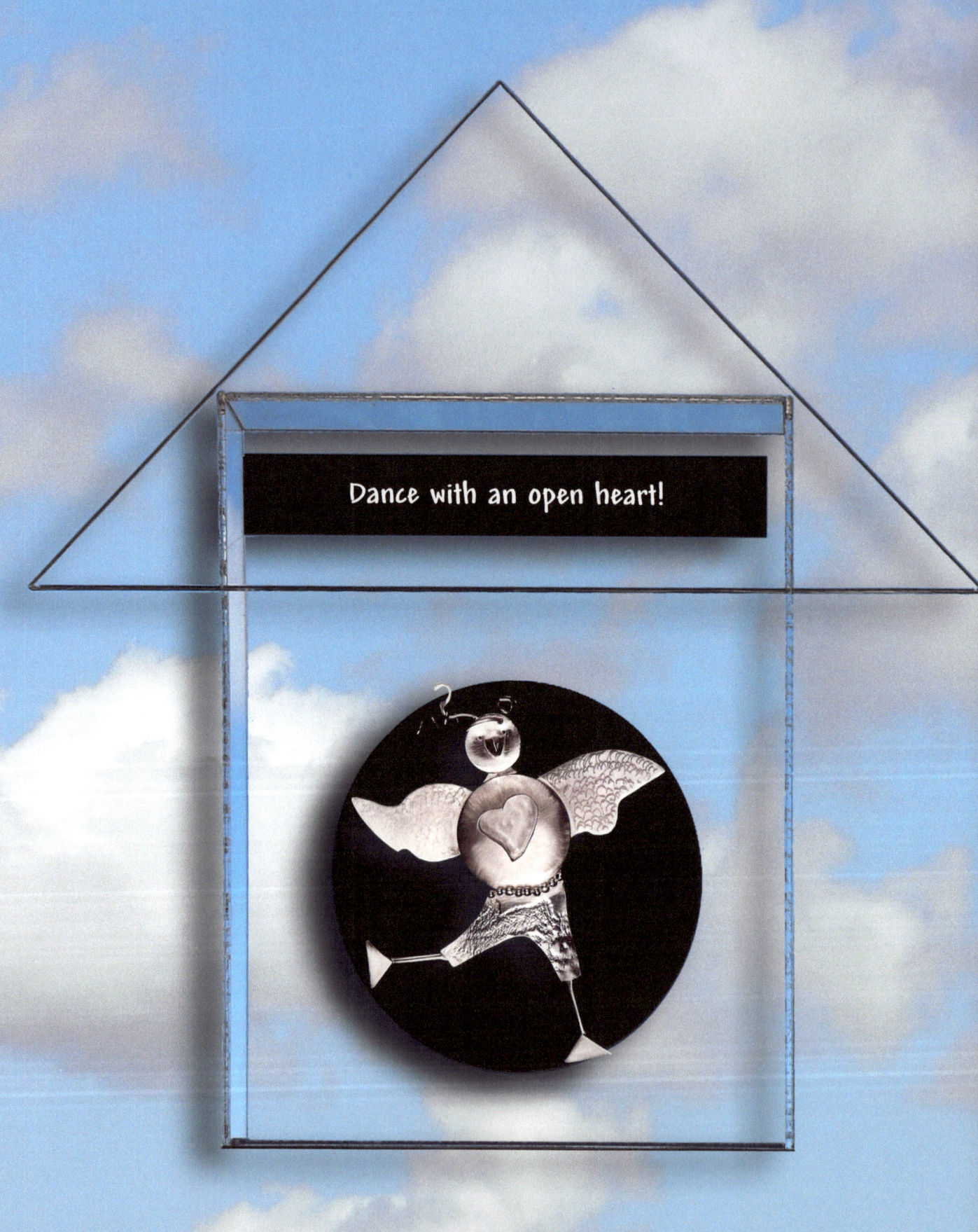

Dance with an open heart!

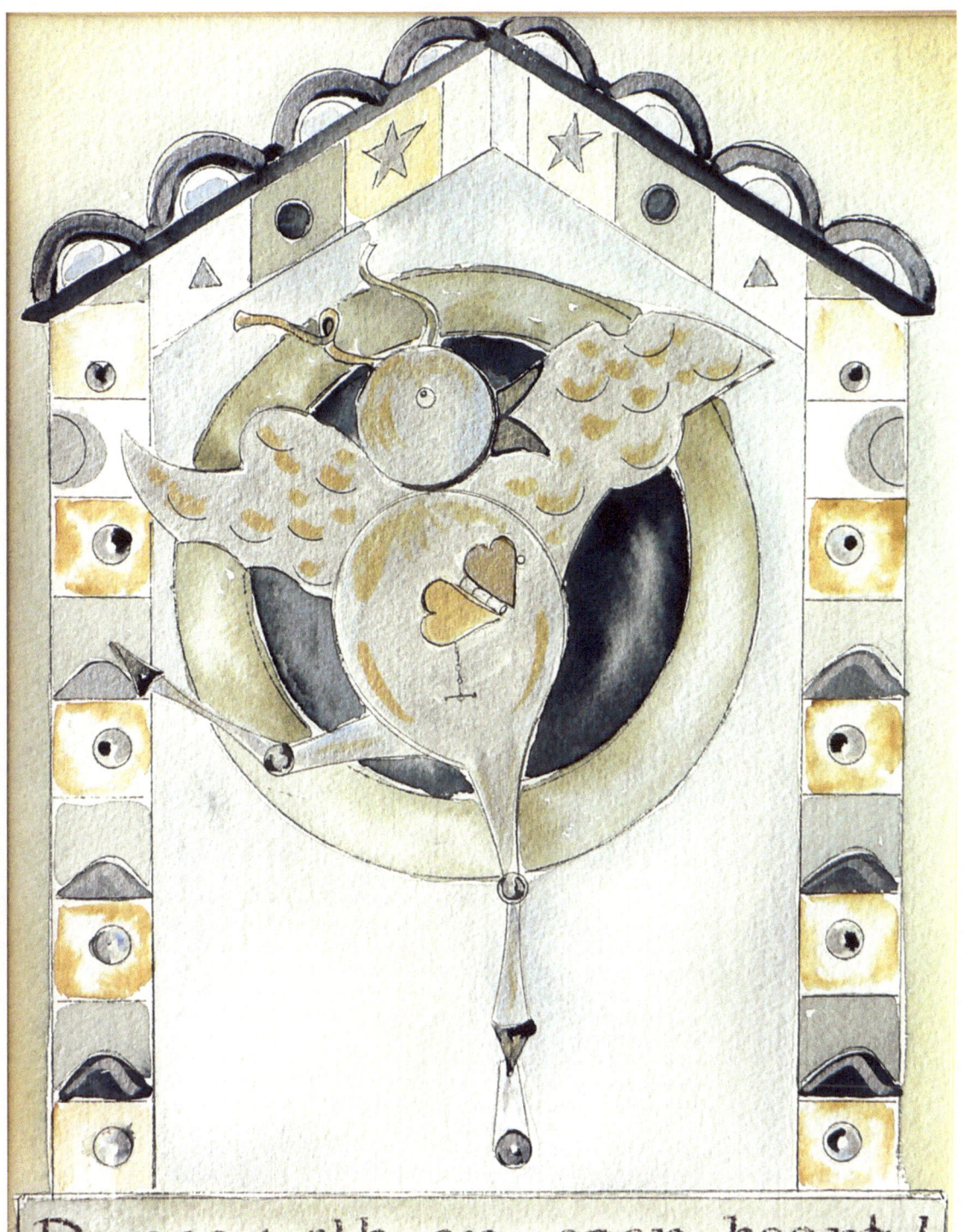

Dance with an open heart!

S. Leuri ...

Possibilities to Prod Your Own Flight of Fantasy

Using the questions listed here in the book, you might respond in writing and discover your own thoughtful answers.

In small groups of friends or family, you could use these questions as a conversation sharing stimulation.

In business settings to tweak some creative thinking, you could use this book to "fly the playful path" or "jump from the perch."

With children or adults this book could be a catalyst for a creative workshop. After being introduced to the thinking here, participants could tap their own innovative ideas and design birds with available materials --- such as mixed media collage---and attach their own words of wisdom. The artist is available to facilitate workshops.

A journaling process could be followed where a bird a day is doodled with abandonment. If you patiently study each drawing, the message should emerge in time.

And it could be that the best purpose these pages serve is to invite you to pause, browse, and smile. That would be enough!

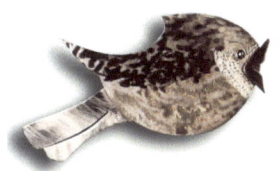
What causes you to sing with joy?

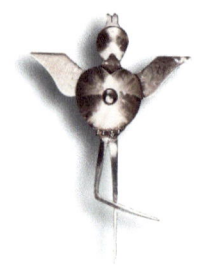

How do you provide balance in your life?

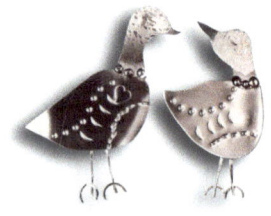

Who are the pals that enrich your life?

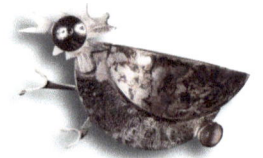

What treasures do you nurture?

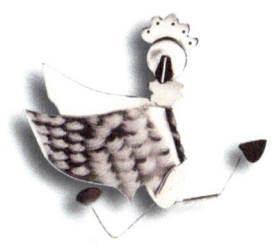

When have you made a courageous leap?

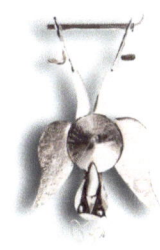

What helps you to "hang in" the difficult times?

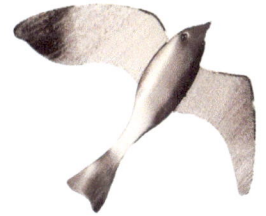

When have you truly "soared'?

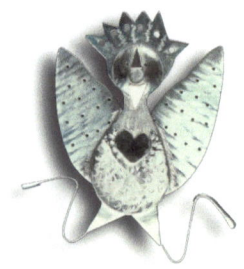

When have you found yourself in unexpected places?

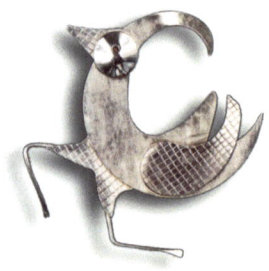

What is the race about?

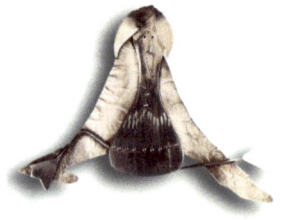

When do you find your energy level really depleted?

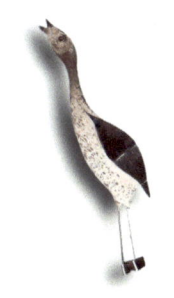

When have you been at your best?

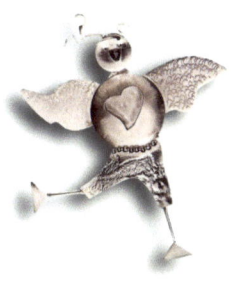

What causes your spirit to dance with love?

See more of Sue Lewis Art with a Visual Voice at www.sukilew.com
Or in the book Vehicles of Inquiry - a contemplative journey.

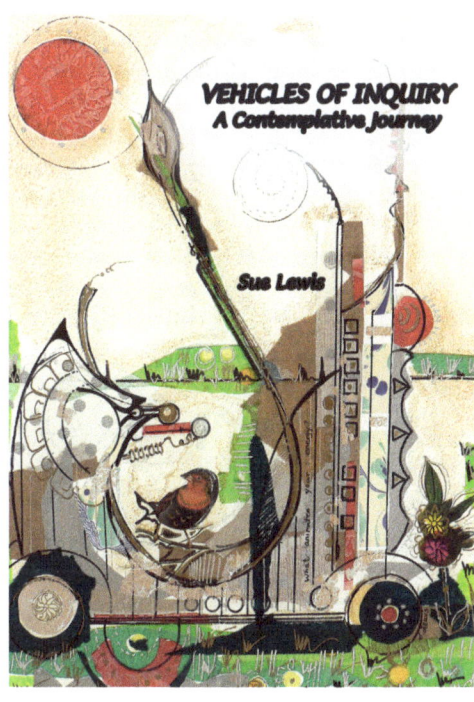

Publication date
May 16 2009

ISBN/EAN13
1442167416
9781442167414

Pages
86

Size
8" x 10"

List price
$20

Available at
createspace.com/3382919

This book has been designed to add a touch of the playful and profound to your own journey. Each vehicle in the book is driven by one of the twenty life search questions. A list of possibilities for using the questions is printed at the end of the book.

Each image is without a rider, inviting you to climb aboard, engage with your own journey, and ponder your responses.

Happy travels!